UNCOMMON PRAYER

Ruth L. Miller

Illustrated by
Martha Shonkwiler

SPIRITBOOKS

Uncommon Prayer
© Ruth L. Miller, 2001, 2007, 2020

Illustrated by Martha Shonkwiler

1st edition published by Peacebringers,
Portland, Oregon, 2001

2nd edition published by WiseWoman Press,
Vancouver, Washington, 2007

3rd edition published by SpiritBooks,
an imprint of Portal Center Press
Waldport, Oregon, 2020
www.portalcenterpress.com

ISBN: 978-1-936902-30-9

With deep appreciation to all the teachers who, in person and in writing, have guided my journey into the world of prayer, this book is dedicated to everyone who is ready to discover the power and potential of their true nature.

Contents

Prayer Is	1
Prayer Does	13
Why Prayer Works	19
We Pray	29
The Prayer Experience	47
A Learned Skill	57
Conscious Prayer	63
Resources	71

Prayer Is

Despite what most of us have been taught for most of our lives,

Prayer is not

words

or actions

or thoughts.

Uncommon Prayer

PRAYER IS A STATE OF BEING

in which we feel connected with, and are open to receiving from, all that is. Certain words or rituals may help us arrive at that state, but they are not the prayer.

PRAYER IS A *FEELING*—

a state of being that comes *as a result of* saying certain words or performing certain actions; it is not the actions themselves.

Uncommon Prayer

The prayer state produces a physiological response in our bodies that is at once electrical and chemical,

A SENSATION OF INNER VIBRATION.

Prayer is a state in which

our thoughts and emotions are in alignment.

Inner conflicts are stilled and we are simply being our essential selves.

Uncommon Prayer

In that state, we experience a different kind of universe than in our normal reality.

In that state, according to Dana Zohar's *Quantum Self*, we are functioning at the quantum level of reality, where

Newton's laws of physics no longer hold.

Our self, usually busy holding this body and mind together while constantly monitoring our environment (keeping us safe in this Newtonian world of matter and energy), stops its scattered busy-ness and coalesces into a single point of awareness. This single-focused self (which Zohar calls a "Bose-Einstein condensate") works as a sort of mind-wave, expanding out in space and time and touching all that is, then collapsing back into "normal" reality when we can no longer sustain it.

This expansion is what Christian mystics have called experiencing the *nunc aeterna,* or eternal now." It's what Eastern traditions have called *samadhi* or *nirvana.*

IT IS KNOWING THE INFINITE.

Uncommon Prayer

Prayer is moving outside the life that has trapped us so that we can participate in creating something greater. It's not asking for more or different "things" in our life. According to the ancient Hindu sacred text, the *Bhagavad Gita (Song of God)*,

> Thinking about sense objects will attach you to sense objects; grow attached and you become addicted; thwart your addiction, it turns to anger; being angry, you confuse your mind; confuse your mind, you forget the lesson of experience; forget experience, you lose discrimination; lose discrimination and you lose life's only purpose.

Effective prayer is an alternative to "thwarting your addiction." When we pray, we have stepped outside of the normal pattern, so we no longer hunger for whatever has driven us in the past. The hunger is satisfied at a level that *in-*

cludes the addiction and so allows us to move beyond it. This is part of the power of 12-step programs and "born-again" Christian healings.

At some level, prayer is going on most of the time. James Twyman, in *Praying Peace,* says that

> our every thought can be prayer.

Whether we realize it or not, we are invoking (calling forth) brief moments of that state of being, and asking for or declaring our wishes and expectations, many times every day. When we say "God, I hope... even leaving out the G*** word—we are praying. Likewise when we say "I wish..." or "If only..." with the same intensity.

Uncommon Prayer

When we long for something, even without words, we are, in a small way, praying.

When we delight in something, feeling gratitude and joy, we are praying—whether we speak the words out loud or not.

Such moments are powerful, but fleeting; they're so brief we barely notice them. The trick is to bring such processes into our awareness so we're participating in the creation of a life that truly serves us—and those around us…

Uncommon Prayer

PRAYER IS THE MOST POWERFUL STATE OF BEING THAT A HUMAN CAN ACHIEVE IN THIS WORLD.

Uncommon Prayer

Uncommon Prayer

All the world's holy scriptures are prescriptions for living life in that state. It's the state that Jesus healed in and was teaching his disciples to reach. It's the state in which the Hindu and Buddhist masters teach and hold *darshon*. It's the state that a shaman works from when healing or divining, as did the ancient Druids and Hebrew prophets.

In that state, we are not our bodies, nor are we confined to the "laws of nature" as we've been taught them. Rather,

WE ARE ONE IN THE CREATIVE POWER THAT SUPPORTS AND

Uncommon Prayer

SUSTAINS ALL THAT IS.

In that state,

WE ARE ONE WITH "THE FATHER WITHIN."

Prayer Does

Current models of our cells' biology tell us that every thought and experience we have is transmitted immediately to the cells of our body. Candace Pert's *Molecules of Emotion* (so impressively illustrated in the film *What The Bleep Do We Know?*) describes how molecules called neuropeptides arrive almost instantaneously at the cell walls when we experience strong emotions or associative memories. A chemical reaction takes place that literally changes how the cell functions whenever these events take place.

Uncommon Prayer

PRAYER CHANGES THINGS IN US AND AROUND US.

More recent studies have shown that the continued presence of these molecules causes the cell to replicate differently, producing "daughter cells" that respond even more readily to them.

Bruce Lipton's book, *The Biology of Belief,* details how the membrane of each of our cells is a biological "semiconductor," working like a computer chip and functioning as the cell's "brain." His research shows that our brain and other cells work as receivers, and that our brains and bodies don't create thoughts and feelings but receive signals and act on them according to the programs we've developed over the years—just like wireless computers.

Uncommon Prayer

When we go through the words and actions we've been taught to call prayer, we are "tuning" the receiver that is our body to a higher frequency. We are increasing the level of vibrations in and between the cells, releasing certain neuropeptides into the bloodstream and sending certain electrical signals to the nerve cells. As we do so, we are aligning our thoughts and emotions, condensing the many aspects of our being into a single "condensate."

In that state, the being we call our self is operating outside of our normal reality.

The cells in our brain and body can receive—and we can perceive—new kinds of signals, at a higher vibration and with new kinds of information. And the cells of our body respond by changing the way they function.

Studies have been done all over the world with people who pray or meditate consistently. Michael Murphy's *The Future of the Body*, and *Calm Healing* by Newman and Miller document dozens of them. The effects of even doing the practice once or twice have been observed as improvements in blood pressure, metabolism, and skin tone, as well as calmer, more effective responses to stress, and improved quality of relationships.

In that state of being,

our individual self

Uncommon Prayer

is not separate

from all others.

As evidenced by the Princeton University Global Consciousness Project during the events of 9-11, and replicated several times since, shifts in states of consciousness by large numbers of people are measurable as a single event. The change is measured as a shift in the operation of specially programmed computers placed around the world. Normally producing endless streams of random numbers, these computers begin to show patterns when large numbers of people think and feel similarly.

The "one mind common to all humanity" that Ralph Waldo Emerson described in his essay "History" responded clearly to the collapse of the twin towers—and again during the 3 minutes of silence a few days later. Intense emotion;

intense focus of attention—both contribute to the power of prayer.

Larry Dossey's *Prayer is Good Medicine* is one of several books summarizing the many experiments over the last several decades that have shown prayer's effect. These studies have demonstrated that

Simply "expressing positive regard" toward a patient, wherever they are, can change that patient's current condition.

Why Prayer Works

Nature is not random. Developments in the "sciences of complexity," such as Chaos Theory, have made it quite clear that Nature is always orderly—even when all we can perceive appears to be turbulence. Mathematicians have found a way to show that there is an underlying pattern in even such turbulent appearances as the Niagara Falls and thunderstorms, in a mountain's rock formations and a coastline's "squiggles," and in all the other natural processes and structures of our universe.

Uncommon Prayer

PRAYER IS ONE WAY WE CAN STEP OUTSIDE OF APPARENT TURBULENCE

> Albert Einstein said, "You can't solve a problem at the level of the problem."

to experience its underlying pattern.

The source of this order, this pattern that underlies all natural processes, seems to be, according to many quantum physicists and cosmologists, the essence of the universe itself.

Uncommon Prayer

In between the stuff
that makes up the
universe,
holding it
all together,
is not empty space,
but a wonderfully rich
"quantum field,"

out of which all matter and energy emerges, according to orderly patterns that most scientists call consciousness or intelligence—and the rest of the world calls "God." Deepak Chopra calls it

"the field of infinite possibility,"

and says that when we achieve the stillness of the prayer state, we are directly participating in that field and helping shape the forms that emerge out of it.

Dana Zohar and other physicists suggest that everything that makes up our universe is conscious, ranging from the simplest subatomic unit to the complexities of the human body. Their research has led many to believe that human consciousness is both a product of universal consciousness and a contributor to it.

Particle physicist Amit Goswami says that the universe is "self-aware," and that this awareness makes up everything in it—including us. Others have suggested that this quantum field has all the qualities of a universal Mind: order, structure, and a capacity to learn and evolve. They suggest that the universal Mind exists in a set of dimensions that surrounds and permeates our space and time.

In their remarkable "trialogue," *Evolutionary Mind,* mathematician Terence McKenna suggests to Ralph Abraham and Rupert Sheldrake that by going "inside," through meditation, contemplation, or prayer, our essential self moves "outside" of our normal space and time. He says that his research points to a new understanding of the nature of mind.

This model suggests that, like a *Star Trek* "worm-hole," our focused imagination, or inward vision, lets us go through our "inside" to get "outside" the limited dimensions of normal space-time and work in that larger consciousness.

our imagination is what allows us to move through to the larger Mind that operates "outside of" or "around" our 3-dimensional experience.

Uncommon Prayer

The great metaphysician of the early twentieth century, Emma Curtis Hopkins, called this

the power of upward vision

Her work with healers and other metaphysical practitioners, combined with her exhaustive review of ancient scriptures and metaphysical and mystery-school texts, led her to teach that

turning our attention toward limitless Mind

Uncommon Prayer

> opens a "beam" by which harmony, order, wisdom, peace, and power begin to fill our awareness.

Based on this principle, Hopkins taught thousands to heal themselves and others, encouraging them to teach what they've learned and experienced, and so demonstrating to themselves and all around them that,

Uncommon Prayer

in that state, thinking thoughts of health toward anyone who appears to be sick will cause that person's body to manifest the order and harmony of Limitless Mind in place of any chaotic appearance of illness.

We Pray

Most of us have been taught to recite a set formula that we've been told is "a prayer." As children, we may have been told to get down on our knees by the bed and recite, "Now I lay me down to sleep... and God bless..." Or we may have learned Hebrew, Arabic, or Sanskrit chants to say or sing as we knelt or sat, lit candles, or broke bread. Or we may have learned Latin chants to repeat as we moved beads on a rosary or watched a priest prepare the Eucharist.

Uncommon Prayer

WE MAY HAVE BEEN TAUGHT THAT SOME PRAYERS HAVE MORE POWER THAN OTHERS.

We may have been taught to recite a specific prayer each day, or at different times of the day, and that we have to use certain words. Some of us were told that "The Lord's Prayer" (or "Our Father") was what Jesus taught his disciples to say

Uncommon Prayer

when they asked how to pray,[1] so we should do the same.

Or, we may have been told that only one word could be used to refer to divine power—and that one must only be said in certain ways under certain conditions. Or we may have been given our own, secret, word or phrase to repeat in a sacred space.

These are important teachings, because, as humans whose minds tend to describe and differentiate, we need some means to still the normal thought processes, and these can help.

---

[1] The "Lord's Prayer" follows the basic outline of the Hebrew "daily blessing," spoken by Jewish men several times a day since long before Jesus was teaching, suggesting that it was not the words but the *mode* that Jesus was offering his disciples. Also, there's increasing evidence that Jesus taught in the local dialect, Aramaic, rather than temple Hebrew—and certainly not in the Greek in which the New Testament was written. So the words may have meant something entirely different to his followers.

The human mind is very slippery and will easily start running around in thought circles if we let it. In fact, it's so prone to do so that Buddhists refer to it as "monkey mind!"

Having something to focus on, something that we've experienced as beautiful, powerful, steadying, or even restful, in the past, helps us to bring "monkey mind" back out of its normal patterns. And we must break out of those patterns if we are to create that alignment of spirit, mind and body, that "condensate," which can move us in "wave form" throughout space and time instantaneously.

WE NEED TO HAVE WORDS AND RITUALS THAT HELP US

Uncommon Prayer

STEP OUTSIDE OF NORMAL THOUGHT INTO A LARGER RANGE OF POSSIBILITIES.

In Hinduism, the whole set of practices called *yoga* was developed over thousands of years to provide different kinds of people with different ways of doing just that. In the West, one type of *yoga* is popular: *hatha yoga*, which focuses on the physical. Several other forms have been developed, as well: *prana yoga*, which focuses on the breath; *bakhti yoga*, the path of devotion; *karma yoga*, the path of good works; and more.

In Buddhism, the art of meditation is practiced as a way to stop one's normal thoughts and achieve a state that is outside of time and space. Many forms of meditation have been developed to accomplish this, each following a different aspect of the mind-body-spirit system. Some fill the mind with a sound or an image; others empty it; still others focus the mind on a process, such as breathing, to still the normal thought patterns and allow the shift.

Christian and Jewish mystics focus on a person or a prayerful phrase, moving deeper and deeper into the experience of those words or that life, until this life and these thoughts no longer call their attention. In that moment,

mystics feel a shift from "ego-centered" life to a

union with the divine, the infinite, All-that-is.

In materialist science, the shift comes through focusing intensely on a problem and its possible solutions, then releasing that focus, doing something else, and sitting quietly or even sleeping, until an insight emerges, fulfilling their desire.

Shamans and Sufis drum and dance and move their bodies and focus their minds until they are no longer thinking normal thoughts and can feel the journey into "the other world" begin.

Across cultures and religions, the specifics may vary, but the essential practice is the same. It's a set of activities designed to shift the mind into that state of being in which normal "reality" is no longer fixed and there is no longer a sense of separation...

Uncommon Prayer

1. Set aside a sacred (the word means "set apart") time, preferably at regular intervals and consistent times of day;

2. Consider why you are doing this, today — what you hope for in your life and world right now — until you feel clear about it;

3. Choose a sacred place, one that allows you to focus on something — an object, some music, an activity — that draws your attention away from your normal thought patterns;

4. Read, chant, sing, or think some 5-50 words that have meaning for you, that you've felt a "thrill of cool fire" when you've heard or said or read them before;

5. Continue to focus and repeat these words for 15 to 30 minutes, returning to them whenever you may be distracted, allowing your normal sense of self to dissolve into the process, and ending when you feel complete.

Uncommon Prayer

This is the basic prayer practice. In general,

the more beautiful the
space and music
and words
that we choose,
the more likely we are
to experience the
"thrill"
and the deeper silence
that goes with it.

Uncommon Prayer

The more senses and emotions we bring to the process—*feeling* the beauty of the place, the power of the word, the body sensations, and the rhythm of the music—the sooner our normal thought processes will stop. (That's why some otherwise materialist-analytic people prefer the "smells and bells" of a traditional mass or orthodox service over the pared-down minimalist rituals of the reform movements.)

Uncommon Prayer

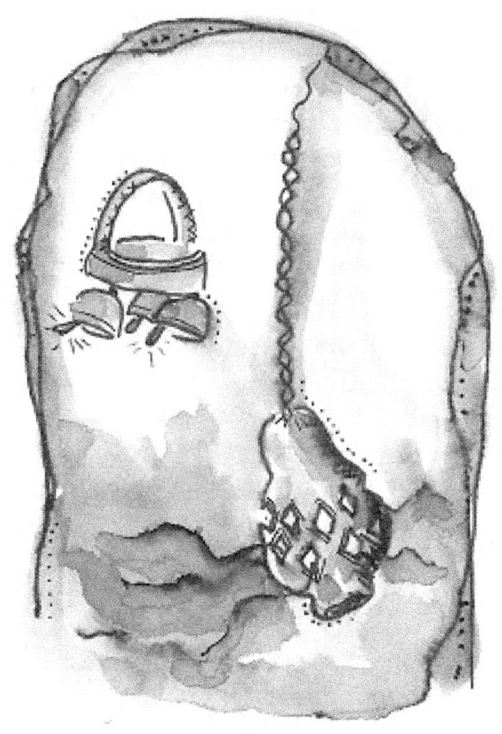

Uncommon Prayer

Doing this regularly has been demonstrated to have remarkable effects. According to scores of studies performed over the last several decades, people who do some version of this practice on a daily basis generally have lower blood pressure, lower cholesterol, more balanced hormones, clearer skin, more effective circulatory, digestive, and respiratory systems, and more physical and emotional stamina and flexibility. They also generally retain more information for examinations, have more satisfying relationships, and heal faster when they encounter health challenges.

Other prayer practices are effective in their own way, as well.

In Christian and Buddhist monasteries, **staying focused on one's spiritual life while doing work that feels like drudgery** has frequently been an issue. The Buddhist solution has been to suggest that the worker think of the dishes or vegetables or floors as "Buddha's body." This shifts one's perspective from thoughts about how mind-numbing the job seems to exploring the love and care one would feel while cleansing the body of the Enlightened One. The Christian tradition has used that approach to some extent, as well—notably in Mother Teresa's work with Calcutta's dying poor, as she experienced each as Christ's body. This practice is particularly useful for those who use service to others as a means for transcending normal thought.

Another approach to the drudgery issue that has worked for many Christians is called "**practicing the Presence**," a method that Brother Lawrence, a monastery kitchen helper for many years, developed as he worked. His goal was to *feel* the energy and wisdom and love of the Holy Spirit moving around and through him in everything he did and said. Over the years, he became so proficient at his practice that people around him could feel what he was experiencing and his company and guidance were sought by many.

A third approach is **repeating a prayer or mantra—a saying that has some uplifting meaning or a sound that reverberates through one's body—throughout the day.** "Lord have mercy," a phrase used by an Orthodox Christian monk a century or so ago, has become popular in recent decades. Variations on *Om* and *Shalom* work for many. Repeating names of the divine is effective for uplifting one's thoughts; Gandhi used the name *Rama;* Hopkins suggests that repeating the words "omnipotent, omnipresent, omniscient" can lift one's spirit to soaring heights.

A helpful guideline in choosing a word or phrase for this practice is to be aware of what various sounds and tones accomplish. An open "Ah" sound tends to align creative, expansive tendencies in the body (most names of the divine are based on this sound).

> *Rosaries*,[2] with their appropriate phrases, such as
>
> ## *Hail Mary, Mother of God*
>
> Our Father who art in heaven...
>
> *Nam Yoho Renge Kyo*
>
> **Om mane padme hum**
>
> serve as useful guides, helping seekers in many spiritual traditions to focus.

---

[2] Rosaries are not confined to the Roman Catholic church. One of the oldest prayer devices in human experience, they are also used by Hindus and Buddhists. (The Dalai Lama has been observed working a bracelet form of the rosary while his teachings were being translated to an audience.

Uncommon Prayer

The Sanskrit term *Aum,* or *Om*, is usually understood to be a completing sound, encompassing wholeness—the fact that the final letter in the Greek alphabet is *omega* supports that understanding. It's worth considering the quality of sound, as well: a piercing musical tone has a different effect from one that is low and rumbling, or one that vibrates in the mouth or chest.

All of these methods have their own advantages—and they can be combined, as well.

In our busy culture, for someone whose work schedule and family responsibilities make it difficult to set aside a period of sacred time every day, the repetitive chores of life can become substitute opportunities to transcend one's normal thought patterns and allow one's consciousness to expand into "wave form." If all else fails, time alone in the shower, at the kitchen sink, in the garden, or at the ironing board can be a day's sacred space,

One caveat: while these unstructured practices can be as effective as a regular sacred time, they require far more discipline to maintain on a regular basis. So for most beginners, they're not usually suggested.

> Many people who are "addicted" to regular, intense periods of athletic activity are, in fact, using those times to stop their normal thinking and to simply *be* in their experience—believing that their workout is the only way they can.

Happily,

...when one has been doing a regular daily practice long enough to feel "the shift" out of normal thought on most days, that "shift" begins to happen during other activities, as well.

The Prayer Experience

This feeling that we're after when we pray is not just emotion. Nor is it just sensation. It's a combination of sensation, emotion, thought, and "gut" sense, or intuition.

IT'S THE FEELING OF KNOWING, IN EVERY CELL OF THE BODY, THAT

Uncommon Prayer

EVERYTHING FITS— IN, THROUGH, AND AROUND US—AND SO IS ACCOMPLISHED.

To get to that feeling is the challenge—and the essence—of prayer.

We start with the words, sounds, movements,

and images
that help us reach a
state of consciousness
in which we can use all
of our senses,
through imagination,
to experience
the desired situation.

Once there, we can begin to experience the emotions that come with having that experience and to sense the reality of it.

Uncommon Prayer

From that state, we open up to the possibility of something more, an even greater possibility, flowing though us into the world. And when we've felt that greater possibility "slip into place" or fit, we begin to feel gratitude for its existence. Then we are truly, consciously, praying.

When a Unity, Religious Science, or Christian Science practitioner prays for a healing, the first step is to turn away from, or deny, the possibility of the disease or lack being brought to them.[3] Then they use whatever technique they know to move them into conscious awareness of the essential qualities of life, order, abundance, and love in the universe.

When they *feel* those qualities as the fundamental truth of the whole, they fo-

---

[3] For more instruction on this process see Hopkins' *Scientific Christian Mental Practice* or Miller's *Unveiling Your Hidden Power: Emma Curtis Hopkins' Metaphysics for the 21st Century*.

Uncommon Prayer

cus that feeling on themselves and the person who has come to them. Then they *feel* the abundant life and wholeness that is the fundamental, and in the practitioner's current awareness, the *only* truth of this person's being.

We reach a point where
a wonderful feeling of
gratitude
flows through
the practitioner's heart
and body:
a heartfelt appreciation
for the wellbeing of all.

Uncommon Prayer

Then the practitioner declares the healing done and expresses thanks to the Living Power of the universe for this opportunity to see and experience it.

Sometimes a practitioner "treats" for a specific thing. One young minister in Chicago felt the need for a warm winter coat. Her first step in the prayer process was to cut out a picture of a coat that appealed to her and put it up where she could see it frequently. Then she wrote a check for what she believed the coat would cost and put it next to the picture. She went a step further and wrote a deposit slip to cover the check and put it next to the check.

Having done all that, she proceeded to imagine what it would be like to have that coat. She imagined putting it on, feeling the weight of it on her shoulders and its texture as she touched it with her hands. She imagined walking outside and "felt" the winter air around her but not touching her through her new, warm coat. She imagined hanging it up in her front closet, ready to put on when needed. In fact, she imagined all of this so vividly that she was surprised not to find it there the next day! She knew she had that coat!

In all that she was doing, she was praying. Her activities were a prayer that recognized the divine as a Presence and Power that sustains and supports us all the time, and expressed a "thank you" for meeting her every need and heart's desire, including this coat.

She went through this imagining/prayer process several times over the next several weeks. That coat (or a better one) was here. There was no doubt in her mind. It was just a matter of allowing it to arrive—and she was *very* grateful.

Then, one day, an unexpected check arrived. It was for precisely the amount that she'd written on her deposit slip!

Uncommon Prayer

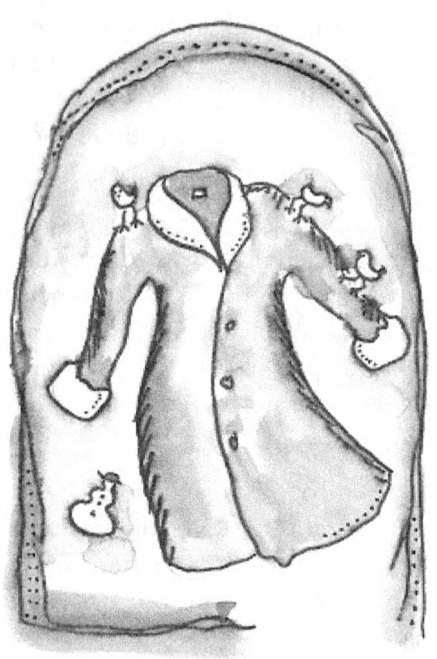

Needless to say, she headed straight to the bank and deposited it, her heart overflowing with praise and appreciation, heading from there to the coat store. And, as she told the story years later, her new coat was everything she'd dreamed it would be.

Of course, prayer is not simply a tool for manipulating the universe to meet our every whim. Rather, it's a way for us to move into a state of being in which we can discover what we truly desire and begin to experience it. As Deepak Chopra has stated,

> "our heart's desires are the seeds of our life's purpose, planted there that we might find our way in the universe."

Uncommon Prayer

IN PRAYER, WE BEGIN TO BECOME THAT WHICH WE WERE BORN TO BE.

A Learned Skill

All the great metaphysicians, including the leaders and teaches of the New Thought and Christian Science movements, have used and taught this approach to prayer. From Ernest Holmes on back through the Fillmores, Emma Hopkins, Mary Baker Eddy, and Phineas Quimby—all accomplished thousands of healings and launched worldwide movements by practicing this process on a daily basis and acting from the insights gained through it.

Uncommon Prayer

When Jesus the Nazarene realized that his disciples weren't able to do the things he taught them to do, he said to them, "Oh, you have so little faith! How long must I be surrounded by people who won't learn what I have to teach?" About his own miracles he said, "These things and greater shall you do." He knew that we all have the capacity to heal the sick or injured, teach the good news of freedom, forgive all error, and revive those who seem to have died; he taught that it's something we all can learn.

In every culture, healers and shamans and mystics and priests have taken on certain likely candidates to be trained for this process. Usually, those candidates have shown no previous indication of intuitive or psychic capabilities, but they have been curious, with a willingness to explore and try things—and to stick to something, even when it may be boring.

Uncommon Prayer

These apprentices are taken through a process of "unlearning" what they had been taught about the world—the "reality" of the solid, the "permanence" of things—and given experiences to help them see what quantum physicists are now discovering: that the universe is a process of movement and energy, and that matter is a temporary form, held in place by the energy of thought and emotion. Then they're offered opportunities to discover their own capacity for changing their world, through various processes—all of which involve the activities which we have called prayer.

Uncommon Prayer

When Shakti Gawain began to teach a similar method in the 1970s, she called it "creative visualization." By separating the creative process from spiritual practice, she made it palatable to our secular materialist business-oriented society, so, by the

1980s, many business schools actually included her book, *Creative Visualization*, on the required reading list. It made a huge difference for many people, empowering them to take a co-creative role in their experience. But *visualizing, while necessary, is not enough. We must bring all of our senses to the process.*

Mind Games, by Jean Houston and Robert Masters, is a remarkable guide that provides a step-by-step process for those who don't believe they can experience an imagined reality with all their senses, or who have difficulty reaching the state of consciousness in which we can do so. Building on the authors' research with shamans and other masters of altered states, the book moves groups of participants through a series of experiences to enhance their ability to imagine with all the senses, and also to expand their normal waking awareness to include more of what's been called "the sixth sense."

Uncommon Prayer

By the end of the *Mind Games* series, participants have not only experienced a variety of altered states, but they have learned to achieve those states almost instantaneously, experiencing with every sense—without the use of any drug or external stimulus. By working through the exercises, in groups and individually, they have experienced virtually every type of imaging process known to humanity. They've significantly enhanced their own mental processes—and they've begun to live in the state that the apostle Paul called "unceasing" prayer.

Conscious Prayer

The process of prayer begins with relaxing the body. We need to have a variety of techniques to help us relax in any situation if we are to be able to move into the prayer state whenever we choose. These may include sitting a certain way, listening to certain music, thinking or speaking certain words, imagining certain images, breathing deeply, etc. The repetitions described earlier can be very useful at this stage.

Uncommon Prayer

Then, since most of us are at least somewhat visual in our imaginings, once we are relaxed we close our eyes and "see," with our mind's eye, the desired conditions, the intended outcome for our prayer—and we begin to "feel" it with our internal senses.

For a healing, we "see" and "feel" the healed person doing things they enjoy doing, full of life and wellbeing.

Uncommon Prayer

For experiencing an event or specific circumstances, we "see" and "feel" ourselves being there, doing it, holding it, using it, and appreciating.

The next step is to become part of the scene we've been imagining. We imagine moving through the space, touching the desired object or holding the person's hand while they enjoy life. We engage the other inner senses as well: imagine hearing the sounds, smelling the smells, and tasting the tastes that go with the experience.

Uncommon Prayer

We continue the imagining until we begin to respond emotionally to it. When we start to feel joy and delight and appreciation for the accomplished event, we're halfway through the prayer process.

When we begin to feel joyful, excited, or happy about what we've been imagining, we may feel the "thrill of cool fire" that Emma Hopkins described as the beginning of knowing that it's complete.

The cells of our body are responding to a higher vibration of energy that is flowing through them as we are bringing our mind, body, and emotions into alignment.

We are forming the "condensate," moving

our consciousness into wave form, which is everywhere in the universe at once.

We need, then, to stay with that "goose bump" sensation. We let ourselves feel the energy flowing through this body and through the scene we've been imagining. We allow it to move in and through and beyond us into the larger world.

We *feel* the world changing.

Uncommon Prayer

Uncommon Prayer

Then we give thanks.

- We *feel* the appreciation and gratitude that is the result of receiving and experiencing our heart's desire.

- We *acknowledge* and appreciate the universe for being what Albert Einstein called a "friendly place," supporting and sustaining us, providing all our needs.

- We *honor* the Power and the Presence that we have felt in the prayer process for moving in and through us and beyond to "give us our daily sustenance."

Uncommon Prayer

Finally, with countless generations of humanity, we affirm our trust and our willingness to move forward in faith and hope, with the age-old confirmation:

AMEN.[4]

For so it is, now and always.

Blessings on your journey—*rlm*.

---

[4] The word *amen* is present in all the Semitic languages: Aramaic, Hebrew, Arabic, and more. It appears to have been part of the Egyptian sacred tradition long before a "god" was given the name *Amun* or *Amen-Ra*. As with all ancient terms, it has several layers of meaning. Most simply, it is "It is done, finished, complete." At its most complex, it means, "On this ground I take my stand and from this point move forward, henceforth." Today, it most often is used as the confirmation, "Yes, it is so."

Resources

Abraham, R., McKenna, T., & Sheldrake, R. *The Evolutionary Mind.*

Chopra, D. *Quantum Healing*

Dossey, L. *Prayer is Good Medicine*

_____, *Healing Words: The Power of Prayer and the Practice of Medicine*

Fillmore, C. *Christian Healing*

Gawain, S. *Creative Visualization*

Goswami, A. *Self-Aware Universe*

Holmes, E. *The Science of Mind*

Hopkins, E. *Scientific Christian Mental Practice*

Masters, R. and Houston, J. *Mind Games*

Murphy, M. *The Future of the Body.*

Newman, R. and Miller, R. *Calm Healing, Medicine for A New Era.*

Zohar, D. *Quantum Self*

The Secret, on dvd

Other books by Ruth L. Miller

On Spiritual Practice:

- *Spiritual Success: a guide for daily practice*
  (published by WiseWoman Press)

On Culture & Consciousness:

- *Mary's Power: discovering the divine feminine in Western culture*
  (published by Portal Center Press)
- *Making the World Go Away*
  (published by Portal Center Press)
- *Home: Choosing Humanity's Future*
  (published by Portal Center Press)

On Metaphysics and New Thought:

- *The Science of Mental Healing: America's Great New Thought Teachers and Healers*
  (published by Portal Center Press)

- *Unveiling Your Hidden Power, Emma Curtis Hopkins' metaphysics for the 21st century*
  (published by WiseWoman Press)
- *Natural Abundance: Ralph Waldo Emerson's guide to prosperous living*
  (published by Beyond Words/Atria)
- *As We Think So We Are: James Allen's guide to transforming our lives*
  (published by Beyond Words/Atria)
- *The New Master Key System*
  (published by Beyond Words/Atria)

Ruth L. Miller, Ph.D. integrates science and spirituality in all her teaching and writings, drawing on her training and degrees in anthropology, environmental studies, cybernetics, the systems sciences, future studies, the psychology of consciousness, and New Thought ministry.
Learn more at www.ruthlmillerphd.com

www.ingramcontent.com/pod-product-compliance
Lightning Source LLC
Chambersburg PA
CBHW052120110526
44592CB00013B/1689